Dear Parent:
Your child's love of reading starts here!

Every child learns to read in a different way and at his or her own speed. Some go back and forth between reading levels and read favorite books again and again. Others read through each level in order. You can help your young reader improve and become more confident by encouraging his or her own interests and abilities. From books your child reads with you to the first books he or she reads alone, there are I Can Read Books for every stage of reading:

SHARED READING
Basic language, word repetition, and whimsical illustrations, ideal for sharing with your emergent reader

BEGINNING READING
Short sentences, familiar words, and simple concepts for children eager to read on their own

READING WITH HELP
Engaging stories, longer sentences, and language play for developing readers

READING ALONE
Complex plots, challenging vocabulary, and high-interest topics for the independent reader

ADVANCED READING
Short paragraphs, chapters, and exciting themes for the perfect bridge to chapter books

I Can Read Books have introduced children to the joy of reading since 1957. Featuring award-winning authors and illustrators and a fabulous cast of beloved characters, I Can Read Books set the standard for beginning readers.

A lifetime of discovery begins with the magical words **"I Can Read!"**

Visit www.icanread.com for information
on enriching your child's reading experience.

The Wildlife Conservation Society and Dolphins

Diana Reiss, who works for the Wildlife Conservation Society (WCS), studies dolphin behavior and was one of the first scientists to tell people that dolphins were being killed in fishing nets. Brian Smith, another WCS scientist, studies river and coastal dolphins in countries such as Thailand, Bangladesh, and India. These kinds of dolphins that live closest to humans are at the greatest risk. Howard Rosenbaum's Cetacean Conservation and Research Program (CCRP) studies species like the Indo-Pacific humpback dolphin and Atlantic humpback dolphin and works with the governments of Madagascar and Gabon to ensure maximum protection for these species. WCS and other organizations are trying to keep dolphins from being killed in fishing nets, improve dolphin habitats, and change rules that make it legal to hunt dolphins.

WCS has managed the New York Aquarium for one hundred years. More than 700,000 people a year visit the aquarium to learn about marine animals such as seals, sea lions, walruses, and dolphins. To find out more about WCS and how you can help dolphins and other endangered animals, visit www.wcs.org.

With gratitude to Peter Hamilton. Special thanks to Dr. Diana Reiss, WCS scientist, dolphin expert, and consultant. Thanks for photographs to Wildlife Conservation Society (front cover, title page, 10-11, 14-15), Marty Snyderman (4-5, 6-7, 9, 12-13, 18, 20-21, 22-23, 27, 28-29, 30-31), as well as Samuel Hung/HKDCS (17), D. Pearlman (24-25), and Diane Shapiro (32).

ISBN-13: 978-0-545-00026-0
ISBN-10: 0-545-00026-2

12 11 10 9 8 7 6 5 4 3 2   7 8 9 10 11 12/0

Printed in the U.S.A.   23

First Scholastic printing, April 2007

I Can Read!

READING
2
WITH HELP

AMAZING DOLPHINS!

Written by
Sarah L. Thomson

Photographs provided by the
Wildlife Conservation Society

WILDLIFE
CONSERVATION
SOCIETY

SCHOLASTIC INC.
New York Toronto London Auckland Sydney
Mexico City New Delhi Hong Kong Buenos Aires

Dolphins whistle and squeak.
They chirp and pop.

4

They make noises that sound
like clicks or claps.
Why do dolphins
make all these sounds?

Dolphins use sounds

to signal to other dolphins.

Each dolphin whistles in its own way.

No two dolphins sound the same.
A dolphin whistles over and over,
as if it is saying, "Here I am!"

Dolphins also show their feelings
with sounds.

An angry dolphin may squeak
or snap its jaw shut with a clap.

It may slap the surface of the water
with its fins or its tail.

Dolphins live underwater,
but they are not fish.
They are small whales.
Whales are mammals.
People are mammals too.
All mammals need to breathe air.

You use your mouth to breathe,
to eat, and to make sounds.
A dolphin uses its mouth to eat.
It uses the blowhole
on top of its head
to breathe and to make sounds.

A dolphin opens its blowhole

to breathe

but must keep it closed underwater.

Inside the blowhole

there are pockets called air sacs.

The dolphin makes a sound
by moving air
from one air sac to another.
If you hold the neck of a balloon
and let the air out slowly,
you can make a sound the same way.

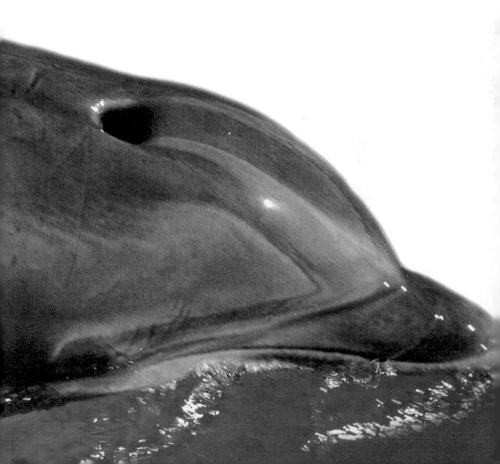

A dolphin makes a clicking sound.
Then it listens for an echo.
A dolphin can hear the difference
between an echo bouncing off a rock
and an echo bouncing off a fish
or a shark or another dolphin.

This is called echolocation.
(Say it: ECK-oh-lo-CAY-shun.)
A dolphin can use echolocation
to find fish to eat
or to tell if a shark is nearby.

There are about 37 different
kinds of dolphins.
Most live in the ocean.
But some live in rivers
in China and India
and South America.
Most dolphins are gray
or black and white.
But two kinds of dolphins are pink!

Most dolphins live in groups

called schools.

Some schools have a few dolphins.

Others have hundreds.

Dolphins in a school help each other.

If one is hurt and can't swim,

other dolphins may lift it

to the water's surface

so it can breathe.

Dolphins like to touch
and pat each other with their fins.
They rub against each other.
They may swim side by side
with their fins touching
as if they are holding hands.

Baby dolphins are called calves.
Calves sometimes play with seaweed.
Or they swim up under a seagull
and knock it into the air.
Grown-up dolphins like to play too.

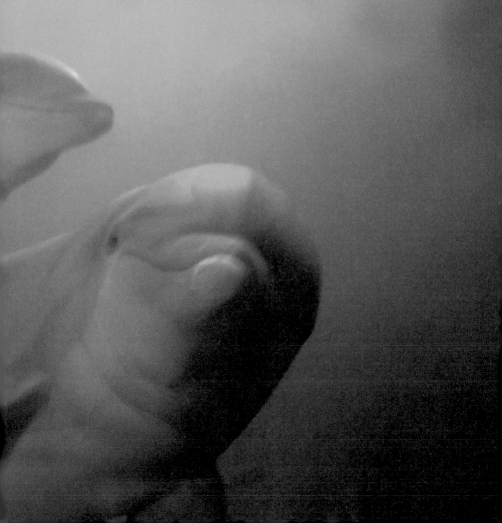

They ride the waves made by boats.
Calves stay with their mothers
for at least three years.
They drink their mother's milk.
Older calves can catch small fish.

Dolphins hunt for fish and squid.
They are also hunted.
Sharks and killer whales and people
kill dolphins for food.
People also catch dolphins
in fishing nets by mistake.

Once, thousands of dolphins
were killed in tuna nets each year.
When people heard about this,
they stopped buying tuna fish.
They asked the government
to keep dolphins safe.

In the United States today,

people who fish for tuna

are not allowed to catch dolphins.

But dolphins are still in danger.

Trash dumped into the water

can make dolphins sick

and kill the fish that they eat.

When people put dams in rivers,

dolphins can't live there anymore.

Scientists go out in boats
to study wild dolphins.
They can tell the dolphins apart
by the fins on their backs.
Scientists count the dolphins
and follow them.

They find out what they eat
and how far they swim.
They try to understand the meanings
of the sounds that dolphins make.

Scientists learn

how we can help dolphins survive.

People helped to save dolphins

from tuna nets.

Now we must protect dolphins
from people who hunt them.
We must keep oceans
and rivers clean.

Then there will always be dolphins,
squeaking and whistling,
swimming and playing,
living in our world.